D1824780

SELLING TO SERVE

HOW TO GIVE MORE VALUE TO YOUR CLIENTS & GET THEM BUYING MORE FROM YOU

By James Ashford

3 5 7 9 10 8 6 4 2

First Published 2016

The Second Edition was published in 2018.

Edited by Eboney Calladine & Penny Barnes

Copyright © James Ashford 2016

Acknowledgements

Every effort has been made to trace copyright holders. The publishers will be glad to rectify in future editions any errors or omissions brought to their attention.

Published by GoProposal Limited Registered in England with Company Registration No: 10004041. Registered Office: 16 Blackfriars Street, Salford, England, M3 5BQ

For more information visit www.JamesAshford.com

TABLE OF CONTENTS

FOREWORD

Occasionally you and I read great books. And very occasionally we see great movies. You're about to get into a really great book.

And let me ease you into it by referencing a great movie (at least I think it was great — particularly the music and its construction.)

The movie in question is The Greatest Showman. And there are several lines in the main musical theme that say it well:

> *It's everything you ever want,*
> *It's everything you ever need,*
> *And it's right here in front of you.*
> *This is where you want to be.*
> *It's everything you ever want,*
> *It's everything you ever need,*
> *And it's right here in front of you.*
> *This is the Greatest Show.*

James Ashford lives his Greatest Show every day and here he urges you and guides to live yours too, with passion and belief.

Let's make it simple — a passionate belief that Accountants change lives AND that the Accounting BUSINESS is that .... a business. And like any business it's really all about people.

James' passion (and that belief) jumps out of every page of this book. It's like any great book — you feel that a) it's written just for you and b) the author is talking to you directly.

So grab it with both hands AND as you do that, grab your highlighter too because it's for sure you'll highlight something on every page — idea after idea, insight after insight.

And as you do that, remember this: the power of any idea is only ever in its implementation.

So don't just highlight. Don't just commit to do. Actually do.

And here's why. Your Accounting Firm can be:

> *Everything you ever want,*
> *Everything you ever need,*
> *And it's right here in front of you.*
> *It really can be Your Greatest Show*

A show you share with people whose lives you change - every second, every day and in every way.

Go for it. You (and they) will be so glad you did.

Paul Dunn | Chairman | B1G1

INTRODUCTION

You are not an accountant, you're a business owner.

But most accountants don't have a business, they have chaos.

And whenever you have chaos, you're unable to spend time on what's important and you'll forever be dragged into what's not important.

You have clients taking up all of your time and energy who don't pay you enough and you're constantly helping your staff with their challenges because everyone has a different way of doing things.

But that's not why you became an accountant.

You became an accountant because you wanted to impact your client's businesses and help them to grow, profitably and sustainably.

But all of a sudden you find yourself as a business owner, leading a team and dealing with challenges you were never told about.

And then the game changed on you. Cloud accounting came along and the work that you were doing, that was valued by your clients, became less so.

And while everyone's talking about this "advisory" piece where you can give the most value, you're still stuck, juggling clients, and managing your staff rather than doing what you love. So you probably feel frustrated and overwhelmed and wonder why every other firm seems to be smashing it out of the park.

Well let me tell you...they're not. Well at least not as many as would have you believe.

But there are a very small number of firms who have been shown the way.

They have their clients dancing to their tune rather than the other way around and these clients are paying 2x, 3x and 4xs more than they were before. They also have their staff all running watertight systems in the way they want them to be run, consistently, every single time, whilst providing incredible experiences for their clients. I know that this is happening because I'm the Director of an accountancy firm myself. I see it happening day in and day out with the accountancy firms I'm helping to achieve the same and it all starts with one thing...nailing your Sales System and with that comes the way that you price and ensuring that you're profitable.

If this isn't absolutely watertight, then you will be losing prospects, losing money and losing control of clients, staff and all other areas of your business.

Your Sales System and the way you price your services is the gateway into your firm and if it's flawed, then the legacy you will experience will be a lack of control, a lack of profits and a great deal of frustration and overwhelming feelings.

Does any of this sound even vaguely similar to what you're experiencing?

If so, firstly, it's not your fault.

Although you spent years studying to becoming an Accountant, you were never told how to run a super efficient, super successful accountancy practice in the advent of cloud accounting and the other accountants, who may have been advising you, are from the SAME world as you, only seeing things from YOUR perspective and perhaps not fully understanding it from their client's perspective.

Secondly, I can help you to solve this problem and I can take away your pain.

How do I know? Because I've been doing it with hundreds of forward thinking accountancy firms who have been bold enough to acknowledge that the world of accounting has changed; accountants who joined the profession, through wanting to provide value and who are sick of it being reduced to a necessity; accountants who are sick of putting up with crap from clients, and not getting paid enough for a service that's so challenging to deliver.

Now we don't class ourselves as an accountancy firm. We're a business, which happens to deliver accountancy services. And this subtle shift of our thinking is important.

This one shift aligns ourselves more with our clients and also gets us thinking very differently to nearly every other accountancy firm out there.

So if you want to think like a business, give more value to your clients AND have them appreciating that value as well as have new prospects turning up ready to buy from you and getting paid more for what you do, then the easiest way to do that is to simply copy what's working successfully in other profitable, successful, chaos-free firms.

And this all starts by getting your systems in place because without those, you don't have a business at all.

You just have chaos.

WHO IS JAMES ASHFORD?

Before we start, I need to tell you a little bit about me so you can understand where I'm coming from and why I'm so passionate about this.

About ten years ago I was made redundant when the recession hit and we had a baby on the way.

I had to earn money fast, so I set up my first business.

I did that so that I could give my family the life that they deserved to have and for us to have more time together.

Only I didn't have a business, I had a job with three assistants.

Then I read a book called eMyth and began learning about systems. But while I knew about them intellectually, implementing them in a way that they stuck, and that everyone did what I wanted them to do, every single time, was another thing. In spite of that, we were successful and profitable, but in the end, that business failed.

It failed because I didn't have the right Sales System or Finance System in my business.

The thing that tipped us over the edge was a series of small financial decisions which compounded over time and left unchecked, took us to the edge.

I know what it's like to sit in front of my staff and say "You know that business you've been helping me to build for the last 4 years. It's gone. It's over. Go home."

I know what it's like to go back to my wife and say "You know all those late nights I worked and things I missed out on because of that business I'd been growing? Well it's over. We need to re-mortgage the house."

I also know what it's like to dust yourself off, pick up the pieces and start again.

As an accountancy firm, YOU have the power to make or break your clients businesses.

YOU are that powerful.

Do you know how many people your decisions impact? Thousands when you think about your clients, their families, their staff, their staff's families, your client's clients, your client's suppliers. There are so many people that are reliant on your client being successful. Their success is directly linked to the finance function that they have in place within their business. So you can't get this wrong (no pressure then!).

Since then, I've become a business systems expert so that I can help business owners to avoid the mistakes I made and build an actual business that gives them the life that they want.

I've been fortunate enough to have worked with over a hundred businesses across many industries, and have helped them to systemise and become more profitable by getting their Sales Systems & pricing watertight and working very successfully.

I have now focused that decade of experience of working with businesses on the front line, into the accounting industry. I'm helping accountants to stand shoulder to shoulder with their clients and to start seeing it from THEIR point of view.

I work with some of the top accountancy firms who employ anywhere between 5 and 50 staff. Helping them to grow more profitably, more efficiently and to totally remove themselves from the day-to-day running of their firm.

But I also work with much smaller firms. Whether it be an army of one or those who just have a few staff around them and who are aspiring to really grow. I show them very quickly how they can increase their fees and ultimately have a greater impact in those businesses they serve.

I typically get accountants doubling, tripling and quadrupling their fees and there are two reasons that excites me:

ONE - I know that you're getting paid for ALL the hard work that you do.

TWO - I know that your clients are receiving the services they need from you to be able to grow, and avoid the experience that I went through when my business failed.

I'm also a Director of My Accountancy Place Limited in Manchester and so all of the systems I help accountants to implement are from the front lines of what's working in a systemised, profitable, efficient and rapidly growing firm of accountants, where the owner is working ON the business and not IN it.

We have been growing by about 50% each year. Half of that growth comes from existing clients and half of which has come from new clients.

So everything I'm sharing with you here works. It has to, because I take my own medicine. I'm a Director of My Accountancy Place and so if the systems and strategies I implement don't work, then I lose too.

My genuine goal and belief is that if I can help accountancy firms to firstly become systemised themselves, to free them up to be able to provide the greatest impact they can with THEIR clients, then we can help businesses to avoid getting into the position I once found myself in.

However accountancy firms can't get anywhere near that and move into this advisory role, UNTIL they have systemised THEIR business and are profitable, efficient, scalable and so that their firm runs without them working IN the business. Because until you get to THAT point, what can you advise your clients on?

You have to get in the trenches with your clients and stand shoulder to shoulder with them as business owners because that's the only way you'll really understand their pain and more importantly, that you can help them to move through that pain.

Make sense? So let's recap...

You are not an accountant, you are a business owner.

Most accountants don't have a business, they have chaos.

And while you have chaos, you're unable to spend time on what's important and you'll forever be dragged into what's not important.

You need a business, which runs on systems, and then you need your team need to run the systems.

The first system an accountant needs to implement and have watertight is the Sales System. Why? Because it's the Sales System where you...

- Make your money
- Start the value exchange with your clients
- Define the value you're going to provide to your client in exchange for the money they're going to pay you
- Take complete control of the client and get them behaving as you want them to from that point forward
- Show that you are the expert on pricing, profits and payment
- Plan out what they're going to be buying from you next.
- Leverage your team and get them doing things YOUR way
- Remove the chaos, the frustration and the overwhelming feeling

At the end of the day, you are a business and the primary function of a business is to make money. And the only two ways you can make money is to get more clients or give more value to the clients that you already have. The only way you can get more clients or give more value to the clients that you already have is by selling your services to them. And as a business, the only way you can do that is to have a Sales System.

So let's begin.

THE 7 SYSTEMS

Accountants love systems and rightly so. But there is one system that is almost always overlooked, and it's this system or lack thereof that cause many of the problems moving forwards.

Before I dive into describing this problem, I want to outline what ALL of the 7 systems are that leading accountancy firms need to have in place, if they are to THRIVE in this new era.

You see, everyone harps on about the fact that you need "systems" in your business, but then fail to tell you which systems you need.

You may have even read "The eMyth Revisited" by Michael Gerber and understand the importance of systemizing and the concept of building the franchise-able model of your business.

But even when they got told what the 7 systems are, the thing that eludes them the most is how to build systems that STICK.

We've all experienced the frustration of introducing a new process to your business only to see it fade away after a short while. That's because the systems that make the processes happen consistently have not been built effectively.

Well I'm going to put pay to that right now.

So let me outline the 7 systems we have in place in our firm and which have helped us to provide greater value, wow our clients and build a scalable business.

1. THE ATTRACT SYSTEM

This is where you identify your DREAM prospects and ATTRACT them in their highest quantity and quality into your firm. If you don't know WHO you want, you can't really complain when you don't get them.

2. THE NURTURE SYSTEM

This is where you connect with those prospects and nurture them over time to the point where they make it clear that they want your services. This is rarely in place and a huge sinkhole of lost opportunities. Our nurture processes are 3 years long for new prospects.

3. THE SALES SYSTEM

This is where you turn a prospect into a client and upgrade existing clients into buying more from you. It's where you define the relationship you intend to have with a prospect, wean out the time wasters, propose to them and convert them into your dream client. Without a sale, no value can be exchanged and so this is fundamental to the growth of your business. This is the one we're going to be nailing in this book!!!

4. THE ONBOARDING SYSTEM

This is where you wow your new clients by making it super smooth to onboard them with minimal pain for them and you. This is their first interaction with your practice and so it's important that you nail it. It's also where you onboard existing clients into new services. We've got this process totally locked down and delivering high levels of wow already.

5. THE DELIVERY SYSTEM

This is everything. This is where you maximise the lifetime value you provide to your clients. It's where you put all of the low level activities on autopilot and free up your accountants to work on their highest and best used activities, with mind-blowing turnaround times and levels of value that are off the scale. Get this right and you will form deep and meaningful partnerships with your clients, where you're an intrinsic part of their success.

6. THE FINANCE SYSTEM

This is where you continually maximize your income by ensuring that you're pricing profitably and have THE most robust payment system that automates the flow of cash from your clients to you. Without this in place, you will be leaking profits, leaving money on the table and the more clients you get, the worse it will be. This system is the one you must be an expert in because it's ultimately where you're helping your clients to achieve success too. But you don't have the right to help your clients to achieve this success until you've mastered it yourself first.

7. THE STAFFING SYSTEM

This is where you attract, recruit and grow the best people that perfectly fit your culture and your aspirations. You can't grow your business, all you can do is grow your people and THEY will grow your business. This only works if you have the robust systems in the first place with NO CRACKS and a clearly defined set of USEFUL core values.

WHY DO WE SYSTEMISE?

There are several reasons why you'd want to systemize your accountancy firm, but most people miss the ultimate reason why we do it.

So let me outline some of the reasons why you should systemise your business and then I'll reveal the BIG one.

1. CONTROL THE CHAOS

As any business grows, it naturally becomes more and more chaotic. You take on more people, learn new methods of doing things, encounter new challenges, get more clients and offer more services and with every new thing we add into our business, the chaos compounds. Systemising your business controls that chaos and returns calm to our lives.

2. FRANCHISE YOUR PRACTICE

Once your business is fully systemised and you have effectively installed the franchisable model into your firm, it could be franchised out. This could be on a large scale or it could just be something you do with a few practices in nearby towns. Creating the franchiseable model of your business is not because you HAVE to franchise, but to give you OPTIONS.

3. SCALE YOUR PRACTICE

Without true systems being installed in your business, scaling would be a nightmare. Each customer you attempt to bring in would widen the cracks, increase the chaos, add to the overwhelm and exaggerate the problems. Some accountants think that if they just push through it will all come good. It won't.

4. REMOVE THE OVERWHELM

Most firms have people running their practice and so they naturally become overwhelmed. This is because PEOPLE should not be running your practice. SYSTEMS should be running your practice and PEOPLE should be running the systems. Do it the other way around and overwhelm will increase.

5. REDUCE YOUR VULNERABILITY

Without proper systems, you're vulnerable because if someone leaves, you're in deep water. But if you have SYSTEMS running your business and that person was running the system, it makes you far less vulnerable. Of course there will be other problems you'll need to deal with but your vulnerability will be less. Proper systems also reduce the risk of someone making a mistake either accidentally or intentionally. There should be sufficient checks in place that prevent your clients, the jobs and key tasks from falling through the cracks.

6. MAXIMISE THE VALUE

Without a fully systemised, crack-free business, there's no way you can be maximising the lifetime value of your clients. Do all of your clients know everything you do? Have you carried out an audit on what services they will need over the next three years? Are there mechanisms in place, which are moving those clients towards those additional services which they need? If not, the great news is that most of this can be automated IF the systems we're right.

7. SELL YOUR PRACTICE

A fully systemised business without the correct technology, automation (where appropriate), instructional videos, manuals and training programs make your business for more saleable AND worth a lot more. A systemised, scalable business can increase the value of your practice by as much as four times that of a normal practice.

THE BIG ONE

So here's the biggy. We systemise our business for one main reason and it's one that is rarely considered by the majority of businesses, let alone accountancy firms.

You should systemise in order to PROVIDE INCREDIBLE EXPERIENCES TO YOUR CLIENTS.

That's it.

That's why we do it.

Your clients will remember how you made them feel long after they've forgotten what you've done for them, and we change the way they feel through the experiences we provide. But we cannot even begin to consider this ultimate level UNTIL we have everything else in place and the service we're providing is incredible and the value we provide has been maximised.

Incredible experiences are where the game is won.

THE SALES SYSTEM

So let me start impacting your business right now by mapping out the blueprint for one of the key systems in your business – The Sales System.

This is the one that is nearly always overlooked and often disliked.

It's disliked because a lot of us have some negative association with selling because of experiences we've had in the past. In particular, selling, especially to highly skilled, highly talented accountants seems beneath them.

What I want to do throughout the course of this book is to reverse that thinking and share with you a totally different approach to selling and help you to discover that it's one of THE greatest skills you can have in your firm.

To sell is truly to serve. It's about understanding your client's weaknesses and discovering how you can strengthen them. It is what allows you to deliver the maximum value you possibly can to your clients.

Without it being firmly in place and fully understood by everyone in your organisation, I guarantee that you will have existing clients who aren't receiving the most value they possibly could from you, AND you will have allowed prospects to have never become clients in the first place.

To sell is your ethical obligation and I will be showing you how, with the correct system, most of the legwork can be done for you so that you don't have to SELL at all. People will BUY from you better levels of service for higher fees and with greater frequency.

But above all of that, the sales system is PIVOTAL in determining the success of the relationship moving forwards. Now that's not to take anything away from the systems before or after this one, as all of them are critical if your practice is to be a success.

But this system transitions a prospect into a client; it takes someone who is already a good fit for you and whom you've been giving value to and turns them into a fee paying client.

It sets the tone for everything to follow and determines the parameters for a successful or doomed relationship.

But before I can properly map it out for you, I need you to reflect on what you have in place now and the challenges that lay around that.

THE TYPICAL SALES PROCESS

Now I use the word 'process' here, because rarely is it what I would call a 'system'. So let me outline how a typical sales process works so you can see the fundamental flaws and the opportunities for massive improvement.

1. INTEREST IS REGISTERED

So typically, somebody registers their interest in your service and raises their hand to say that they want to talk to you about you providing the accounting function of their business.

This hand raising may come in the form of an email or a phone call but normally sounds something like this:

"Hi, I have a business and I'm currently looking for a new accountant. I've checked out your website and wondered what you charged? Could we have a chat to discuss? Cheers, James"

2. A MEETING IS ARRANGED

Then what happens is you may call them or reply to the email and you may even ask them a few questions, but essentially you arrange a meeting to discuss their requirements.

3. THE MEETING OCCURS

Then in around a week's time, you have an hour-long meeting where you learn more about their business and perhaps even deliver a presentation.

You may have some standard questions, which you ask...or you may not.

You may also have some sort of pricing tool which can give them a good indication of costs there and then...or you may not.

You then promise to send them a proposal outlining costs which you then email to them over the next few days.

4. A PROPOSAL IS SENT

You then spend time producing the proposal and a letter of engagement which outlines the costs and scope of the work you plan to do for them.

You send them through...with your fingers crossed.

This whole process normally takes longer than you promised the client it would and the documents are perhaps not as thorough as you'd like them to be.

The proposal is also probably not a compelling sales tool that wows the client, but hey ho, it's done.

5. YOU FOLLOW UP

At an undetermined time in the future, you or a member of your team then calls to see if they want to go ahead, which they either do or they don't.

If they don't, well not to worry. We won't chase them because we're not sales people right and we don't want to be seen as pestering them?

If they do, we sign them up.

6. YOU SIGN THEM UP

Now I'm confident that you will have some sort of technology in place that permits an online sign up. If not, then that's something you certainly need to sort out.

So let's assume you have that in place.

This normally then requires some manual step of taking the costs from the proposal and sending it through to prospect to be signed electronically...which they hopefully do.

If they don't sign, you'll probably give them a nudge at some point...probably.

And that's it.

That's the normal process and it seems reasonable enough right?

Wrong.

And it's so wrong that I would anticipate that if your process sounds familiar to this, then you are creating yourself a whole world of pain further down the line.

WHAT'S WRONG WITH THIS PICTURE?

Let me break this down, outline the major problems with this process and share the proven blueprint for nailing it.

1. THE INITIAL INTEREST

So somebody registers his or her interest in your service. THIS is the one moment you have to take control of the situation. It's the only chance you have to stamp your authority on the relationship and reassure them that they have just found THE expert that can provide what they're looking for. You have one chance to nail this.

2. ARRANGING THE MEETING

They want a meeting with you, but the problem with that is...you don't know at this point if YOU want a meeting with them.

What's the point of tying up your precious accountant's time if you don't know if they're precise fit for your firm and whether or not you can provide them with incredible value.

So you need a step in here that determines this fit, removes the time wasters but also doesn't scare off your dream customers. The balancing act in getting this right is pivotal in making the rest of this system work.

But let's say they get past that phase and everything seems rosy. What typically happens between arranging the meeting and having the meeting is...nothing.

Sure you might be forward thinking enough to send out a reminder email. Hell, you may even by firing out SMS text reminders, but typically that's it.

This is a massively wasted opportunity to start the selling of your services.

Why waste the time between ARRANGING the meeting and HAVING the meeting, to move the relationship forward.

Wouldn't it be a different situation if this prospect, was turning up to BUY from you rather than to be SOLD to.

And what if that all occurred automatically, without you having to lift a finger?

So assuming you don't have that, this time is wasted and it's time you don't have.

3. THE MEETING

So normally, a senior member of the accounting team conducts the sales meeting. Their goal is to take them from 0 to 100 in the space of an hour (0 is where they don't really know how we can help them and 100 is where they're signed up).

So we've tied up one of our most valuable assets to complete a near impossible task...but it get's better.

This senior accountant is then going to spend the next 40 minutes trying to figure out what's going on in their business and what challenges they're facing. They will go on to attempt to sell a collection of services and try to sell the benefits of each one to the prospect.

Now if you're worth your salt, you should be charging a fair whack for what you do, certainly more than the competitors. So you have this uphill struggling of pitching something more expensive than everyone else to someone you know little about.

But if you're unable to agree fees, produce a proposal and produce a letter of engagement there and then, you won't be able to agree anything, so you have to let them go.

You then haven't confirmed when you can call them next, so you are now relying on the hope that you will perfectly be able to guess when they'll be ready to make a decision.

4. THE PROPOSAL

Now comes the fun part.

That proposal that you said you'd have by the end of the week has taken a little longer than you anticipated to produce. So it gets sent out with a semi-plausible excuse as to why it's late. This annoys the hell out the prospect and is the first promise broken.

The ability to command high fees is now on shakier ground than before, but the process continues.

This proposal outlines the costs and…well that's it, it outlines the costs and this proposal looks like every other proposal that every other accountant has ever sent, because a proposal's a proposal right? Wrong.

This proposal is your salesperson in the room after you've walked out. This proposal now has a job to do, and if it's not designed to nail the deal, then you're going to be losing potential dream customers. If you got this right, as well as convincing them to sign up for your services, it could also be encouraging them to sign up for MORE services.

They don't just need YOU to upsell them...they could upsell themselves.

5. THE FOLLOW UP

The follow up is where most accountants allow money to literally trickle through their fingers. Firstly, you need to know exactly WHEN to follow up. You can't be leaving this to chance.

You needed to have known who else they needed to have spoken to and how long it would take them to make a decision and then after that, you still need a long-term follow up process in place, because what if they're not ready to sign up this year? What if they want to stay where they are for 12 more months because their accountant's their friend and they don't want to upset them (yeah, let's see if you're still friends when you've left them.)

So it's fair to say that the follow up doesn't occur and if it does, it doesn't occur well.

6. THE SIGN UP

So this process for many accountants (If you have it online) appears fairly robust and in isolation, it probably is.

But it falls down in its ability to smoothly transition someone from WANTING to sign up to actually SIGNING UP because there is normally a manual process in creating the Letter of Engagement.

This may delay the process by a day or maybe longer.

Where it can fall down is if they DON'T sign. What then? What mechanisms do you have in place to ensure that it DOES get signed?

If it does fall down, the system then typically breaks again and reveals another crack, as there is normally time lost between signing up and your ONBOARDING SYSTEM kicking in, presuming you have one.

Now maybe this doesn't all seem that bad, but there are further problems that this then creates...

IT GETS WORSE....

There are additional problems that are created in this process that may not have been evident at first glance.

Firstly, the whole process is drawn out and prevents the right person from signing up there and then. You can go out and buy a car today or even a house. Why not accountancy services?

Secondly, it ties up some of the most knowledgeable and senior members of your team, whose time could be better spent elsewhere.

Thirdly, there is a disconnect between the promises sold during that sales meeting by the Senior Accountant and the service that then ensues and which is typically delivered by someone else once they've signed up. This typically leads to a sense of underwhelm for the client and overwhelm for your accountants.

You are also restricted with the amount of sales meetings that can take place because you only have one or two people who can deliver an effective presentation and pitch.

The whole experience for the prospect doesn't leave them feeling wowed. This makes it more challenging to sell them what they actually need for the fees they need to pay.

But all of this...all of these problems pale into the background when you understand the enormity of the major problem that it compounds.

A problem which is undermining your entire firm, causing all of your accountants to feel overwhelmed, minimising the value you can provide to you clients, increasing your churn rate, reducing your profits, restricting your referrals and basically causing 80% of the headaches throughout your firm.

THE REAL PROBLEM

The real problem you've just created is in allowing the prospect to take control of the process and to behave how THEY want. You have relinquished all authority throughout the process and handed the power to them.

The knock on effect is that if you're lucky enough to sign them as a client (and the above method is based on luck and hope) they will continue to behave as they want to and to take control over the relationship. It's a bit like how the alpha dog in a pack of dogs is chosen.

None of them actually wants to take the lead because it's risky, but one of them has to and so one of them will, even if it's not the strongest. Your client is now in total control of the relationship because of how YOU allowed it to be formed.

So when they don't reconcile their accounts on time, or they fail to raise those invoices and they rock up in your office with a carrier bag of receipts and tell YOU to sort it out...you can't really complain.

When your accountant's precious time is taken up chasing these clients, increasing turnaround times and preventing you from delivering higher value services, you can't really tell your client off.

When your client then turns round and says the value you're providing me is not what you promised, you're terrible, I'm off... you can't really blame them.

But let me get you off the hook too, because you're not to blame either.

I'm sure you're a great accountant.

I'm sure your intentions are good and that your genuine goal is to provide great value to your clients.

It's just that the world has changed and your competition is no longer other accountants.

Your competition is anyone I choose to compare you to.

So if I've been onto Amazon's website on a Saturday night and ordered a book and it arrives the following day...on a Sunday morning and then I come and meet you and it takes you a week to send me a proposal...rightly or wrongly, fairly or unfairly, I'm comparing you to Amazon.

If I've just been to Virgin Travel that morning and then meet you in the afternoon...rightly or wrongly, fairly or unfairly, I'm comparing you to Virgin.

You now need to be thinking about being WORLD CLASS, not just the best accountant in your town, because your clients have more power and higher expectations than ever before.

You need to be able to maximise the lifetime value you bring to them and deliver it through world-class experiences...or you're going to lose to someone else who does.

The massive problem you created started when you first allowed the prospect to take control of the process.

The good news for you, is that this process is easy to correct it can run largely on autopilot and has already been proven to work in other accountancy practices.

I have the blueprint...and I'm going to share it with you now.

THE BLUEPRINT

What I'm about to share with you is a gift.

It's what's been learnt and refined by being in the trenches and making this work and now I'm revealing it to you.

It is woven with many gems that can have a real impact on the way you sell your services, so please look out of them and take all you can from it.

Before I dive into the details, let me just give you the Sales Process Blueprint for you to refer back to, so you don't get lost.

If you'd like the poster version of this to print out, pin up, scribble on or whatever, just go to www.JamesAshford.com/blueprint

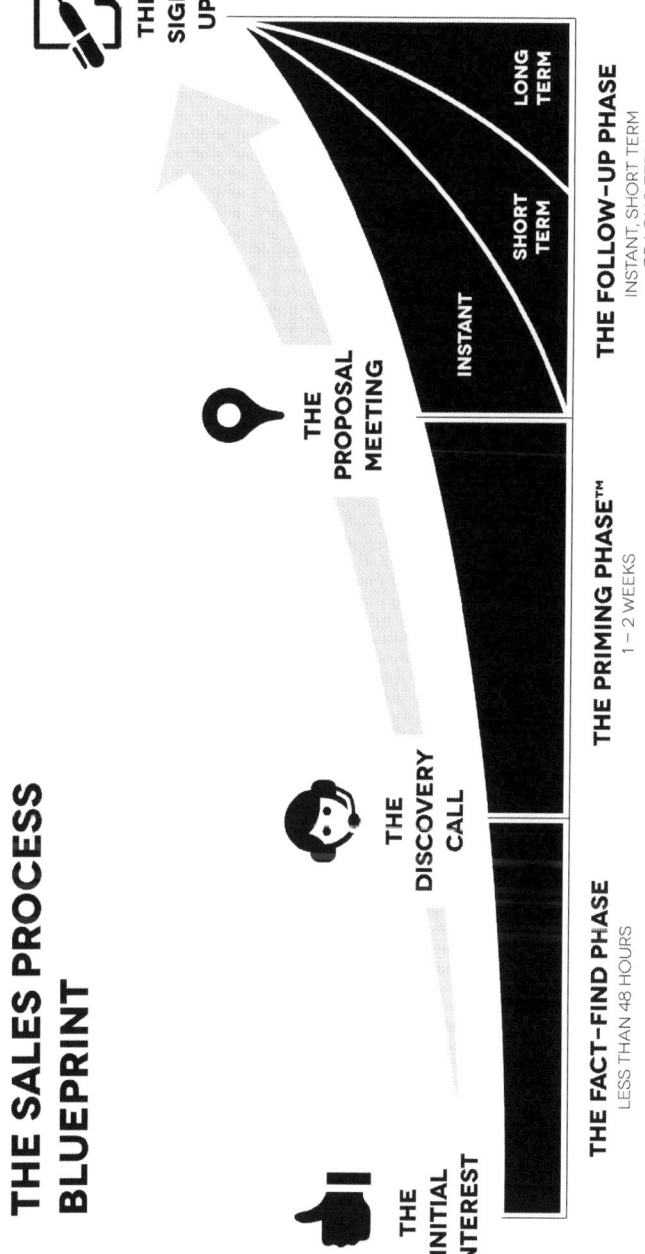

THE SALES PROCESS BLUEPRINT

THE INITIAL INTEREST

THE DISCOVERY CALL

THE PROPOSAL MEETING

THE SIGN UP

THE FACT-FIND PHASE
LESS THAN 48 HOURS

THE PRIMING PHASE™
1 – 2 WEEKS

THE FOLLOW-UP PHASE
INSTANT, SHORT TERM OR LONG TERM

INSTANT

SHORT TERM

LONG TERM

1. THE INITIAL INTEREST

When the initial interest comes in, you must, must, must take control. They need to know that they've just discovered the expert.

They need to feel your stamp of authority and regardless of how this comes in or who first takes the call or email, you've got to leap straight into action and take control. You've got to wow them because these people are in pain.

Imagine if you went to a hospital with a life threatening injury and you were greeted with someone who said "Erm...I'm not sure what to do, let me find out."

NO!!!

You need someone who, in their opening sentence, fills you with reassurance that your injury will be treated and your pain removed.

This comes down to clearly mapping out your process, scripting different possibilities and conducting regular training around this.

What you want to be doing is transition them into what we call the Discovery Call.

This is a 15 minute phone call that ensures you're a good fit for each other and is a chance to gather some powerful information that we're going to use later in the process.

So there are a few different ways in which their interest could be shown to you...

THEY'VE EMAILED YOU

So if they've emailed you and provided a phone number, you could call them and take them straight into the Discovery Call. Or they've emailed you and haven't provided a phone number, in which case you either need to request it or send them a link to your online appointment scheduling software.

THEY'VE CALLED YOU

If they've called you, then we're straight into the Discovery Call anyway, which is great. If they don't have the time to talk then, book the Discovery Call at that point, but if they are ringing then chances are they have the time to speak to you now.

THEY'VE FILLED OUT A FORM

If they've filled out a form on your website (which is quite common) then we take them on a slightly different journey.

1. They complete the simple web form
2. They are then directed to a video explaining that the next thing they need to do is to arrange a Discovery Call with you and what that entails.
3. On that page they are able to book an appointment straight into your Client Coordinator's diary using something like Appointment Core, Calendly or ScheduleOnce.

4. They then receive a confirmation email thanking them for arranging the call and outlining what it will involve and what questions we'll be asking them on the call.

5. You then direct them to another short form where they then answer some simple questions ahead of the call. We call this the FACT FIND PHASE and we use it to find out their Annual Revenue, No. of employees and when their year end is, if they're happy to share that with us of course.

6. They then receive a confirmation email and or text on the morning of the call, reminding them of times and what they can expect on that call.

Now this might seem like a million miles away from where you are now, but with the right systems and the right technology, this is a relatively straightforward process to install.... and not only does it run on autopilot, it WOWS!!!

YOU'RE CONTACTING THEM

So you may have been handed a referral, in which case you're contacting them.

If you're emailing them, you could direct them to your online booking link.

If you're calling them, you can either take them straight into a Discovery Call if appropriate or use that call to book the Discovery Call.

Whatever happens, they don't get to have a Proposal Meeting without first having a Discovery Call.

This is YOU taking control.

Business is a game and this is YOUR game... your rules.

If they want to play with you, then they have to play by your rules.

2. THE DISCOVERY CALL

The Discovery Call is a 15-minute call done over the phone.

Its purpose is to establish you as the authority, to discover critical pieces of information about them and their business and if a good fit, to arrange the Proposal Meeting. This would be done by your admin staff, which we call the Client Coordinator.

I would develop a clear script and then train those members of staff in how to deliver it efficiently. I will give you an example of this.

We also want to capture certain information, which you would need to store in an appropriate CRM system. we use Infusionsoft for this because not only does it store the data, but it also triggers off automated emails, text, letters and tasks on the back of it. It also naturally feeds into the next system you need in your business, which is the Onboarding System. But we'll save that for another time.

Now dependent on how you tackled the Initial Interest and Fact-Find Phase, you may have already captured some of this information. If so, cool.

So let's dive into what a call might look like and the questions you need to ask.

Now you might not use scripts in your business currently. You might think that training your staff in how to follow scripts is too granular. You might be more of a freestyle kind of business than that.

Well all I can share is my real world experiences in using scripts and training teams to stick to them and to evolve them and... THEY WORK. They create scalability, consistency, wow and free you up from being involved in the process.

Some of my most successful clients devote half a day every week to staff training of which role-playing based around scripts plays a key part.

THE SCRIPT

So let's say James from Acme Limited has booked onto a Discovery call via a web form on your website...and Amy is calling them to deliver the call

Hi James,

My name is Amy and I'm the Client Coordinator here at My Accountancy Place.

Thank you for arranging a Discovery Call with us.

This is an opportunity for us to learn more about your business, understand what's working well, the challenges you're facing and how we can help you to overcome those challenges.

I will then answer any questions you have and if we think we're a good fit for each other, I can arrange a Proposal Meeting with one of our Senior Accountants.

How does that sound?

Great

Firstly, I need to get a feel for the size of your business so that if we do choose to move forwards with a Proposal Meeting, I can arrange that with the accountant who will be able to best serve you.

    A.   So what prompted you to reach out to us?

    B.   What's working well in your business?

    C.   What challenges are you facing?

    D.   What is your annual revenue?

E. *How many employees do you have?*

F. *What current accounting software do you currently use?*

G. *On a scale of 1-10. How would you rate your current accountancy function?*

H. *What would make it a 10? (this is an amazing question because it arms you with the precise information you need to convert this prospect into a client)*

I. *When is your year-end?*

J. *What questions can I answers of yours?*

[ANSWER QUESTIONS]

Fantastic, so I believe we could certainly help you with those challenges and help you to grow your business in the way you've described.

The best accountant to help you to achieve your goals would be Paul Bell because he has a lot of experience with helping businesses of your size to achieve the goals you've described here.

So the next step would be for me to arrange a Proposal Meeting with him if that works with you.

This is where Paul would be able to go deeper into your business and your challenges and give you some real value during that meeting.

This wouldn't be a big sales pitch. We actually make it a valuable experience for you by showing you how you can take your accountancy function to a 10, and outlining the blueprint for making that work

We will then show you what that would look like if you wanted us to provide that function from an investment point of view and we will actually produce an instant proposal for you.

If you're happy with that proposal and you want to proceed, you will be able to sign-up there and then. But there will be no pressure to do that.

In order to make that meeting the best use of your time, there's just one video I'd like to send you to watch BEFORE that meeting.

This outlines how we work and would save us from having to talk about ourselves during the meeting. That way we can focus all of our attention on you and impacting your business from the outset.

Does that sound good?

[ARRANGE MEETING]

So I'm now going to send you confirmation of your meeting with a link to the video.

If you have any questions at all, then please call me back.

Thank you and we look forward to meeting with you soon.

This is the type of script you may deliver on your call. You of course need to put it into your own style and so here are just a few pointers...

- I would avoid being pulled on price during that call. You could give a 'from' price to ward off time wasters, but we really want to be able to establish the value during the Proposal Meeting. Your fees may be double what they're currently paying, and if you haven't had chance to communicate the value of your service to them, you could be losing potential clients.

- We don't allow them to ask questions at the start. This hands control back to them. They can ask their questions at the end...if appropriate. If they are insistent on asking their questions, then I would write them down, acknowledge that you WILL answer them, and then proceed with your call as scripted.

- We ask the *"What would make it a 10?"* question, because this arms you with all the information they need to nail the deal. It also prevents you from taking about things which are irrelevant to the client.

- We sell them on the idea of watching the video BEFORE the meeting. This is a critical component of the whole process, as you'll see. With some clients, we've even gone to the extent of telling them that if they don't watch the video, then we'd have to rearrange the meeting, as it would be a waste of their time. This is a judgment call but very effective in establishing authority.

- But the principle in play here is that if they're not prepared to watch a 10 or 20 minute video, what chance do you have of them reconciling their accounts or signing up for the package that you're going to want to sell to them.

3. THE PRIMING PHASE™

THIS is a game changer.

So what typically happens is the Proposal Meeting is arranged and then what happens between that booking and the meeting???

NOTHING.

This is a massive waste.

In our firm, we call this the Priming Phase™ and we use this time to pre-sell our services BEFORE they even turn up to the Proposal Meeting.

If you get this right it takes none of your time and when they arrive they will turn up ready to buy from you, rather than to be sold to.

The length of time of the Priming Phase™, would determine the amount and type of communication we would send out. But for this illustration, let's say it's one week.

THE CONFIRMATION EMAIL

As soon as the Proposal Meeting is arranged, you send them their confirmation email and in this email you should embed a video, which would typically done by the owner of the firm or someone who is good in front of camera.

This initial video is to thank them for booking the Proposal Meeting and to quickly outline what to expect during that meeting. It's then to reiterate the importance of watching the next video, which will be sent out tomorrow. This initial video is only very short let's say between 1 to 2 minutes long, but it starts to train the client in watching your video content and more importantly…taking action of the back of it.

THE PRIMING VIDEO

The very next day is when we're going to send out an email that contains the main Priming Video.

But before I outline the content of this video, let me explain where this idea first originated.

I met My Accountancy Place and the owner was a very enthusiastic and passionate business owner called Paul Barnes.

He was awesome in Proposal Meetings and would nail the deal 9 times out of 10. But this created a few problems. In every meeting, he would be going through the same points. This is inefficient and was actually taking up several hours of his time each month.

Not only was this inefficient for Paul, but it was also inefficient for the prospect, because 10 or 20 minutes of that meeting was being taken up with information, which although important, was not terribly valuable to the prospect.

Also, if Paul was to scale his business and to focus on the areas, which needed his attention, he couldn't be involved in every Proposal Meeting. We needed to better leverage Paul's time.

The other problem that was being created was between the promise that he was selling to the clients and the delivery of that promise by someone else i.e. his accountants (or Client Finance Directors as he calls them.) Because with the best will in the world, it's difficult to communicate EVERYTHING you discussed together and the promises you made, to the person who you now expect to deliver on those promises.

So we developed this idea of filming Paul, going through all of the amazing points he makes in those Proposal Meetings. We filmed it once and embedded it into an automated email sequence which goes out to the prospect once their Proposal Meeting is booked.

By doing the above, this has...

- Massively freed up Paul's time to be working on his business rather than in it.
- Allowed his Client FD's to attend the Proposal Meetings instead of him and for them to make the promises, which they are going to be delivering on.
- Primed the client before they even turned up to the Proposal Meeting and pre-sold them.
- Freed up time in the meeting, which the Client FD could use to give value to the prospect and to actually invest in the relationship before any money has changed hands..
- Increased the average proposal value from £250/month to £450/month
- Produced a scalable process that has increased the value of his business if he ever came to sell it.
- Started to turn his firm into a franchiseable business.

We use Infusionsoft to automate these processes, as it also allows us to 'set and forget' and also track whether they've watched the video or not.

If you know whether they've watched the video or not, you could send a polite email before the meeting if they haven't watched the video, suggesting that the meeting should be rescheduled.

This is really taking control of the process.

It can be politely sold to the prospect on the premise that the meeting would be a waste of their time as we won't be able to deliver the most value we possibly can to them.

What it really does is indoctrinate that person into playing by our rules...or don't play at all.

This may seem harsh at first, but let it sink in. The theory is sound and it works.

So let's get back to the content of this Priming Video.

A great video should...

- Be very conversational, unscripted and natural.
- Describe your story and why you're so passionate about giving great value to your clients.
- Outline how the Proposal Meeting will work in more depth and specifically explaining that they will be given a Proposal during that meeting, which they can sign up for there an then if that's right for them to do.
- Encourage them to bring any decisions makers to that meeting. We want them turning up to buy from you. We're not going to be pushy in the meeting but if they're ready

to rock, they should be allowed to...we don't want to have more meetings than necessary.

- Bring in testimonials from other clients in the forms of words on screen or even as video snippets, if you want to be that adventurous.

Now all of this might sound like a lot of work but it doesn't have to be. Also don't forget, you are only doing this ONCE so you never have to do it again.

If you are looking for a game changer, then this is it.

THE FINAL REMINDER

On the day before the meeting you should then send out a final email reminder.

If they haven't watched the Priming Video yet, this is where you can suggest that the meeting be rescheduled or at least acknowledge the fact that if they haven't watched the video yet and suggest that now would be a good time to do it.

This is also another great chance to wow them.

For example, do you send directions in your confirmation email?

Ooooh, you do? Nice one. But do you send a Directional Video?

No.

A Directional Video is where you produce a short film that shows them exactly where your offices are, how and where to park, how to get into your building, which door to knock on or what buzzer to press.

This amazes prospects and is so easy to do.

You could just do this with your smart phone and top and tail it with an animated logo which you could buy off Fiverr.com for... well a fiver.

Wowing your prospects has never been easier.

In this email, you also want to outline what the Proposal Meeting entails again, the fact that they'll be getting a proposal and to again encourage them to bring any other decision makers.

If you want to see an example of this video in action, go to www.JamesAshford.com/reminder

4. THE MEETING

So if you have the correct systems in place, then your accountant should now be armed with everything they need to deliver great value to the prospect during that meeting. That prospect should be turning up excited, wowed and primed, ready to BUY.

So let's say for argument's sake that your meeting is 1 hour long. The first 40 minutes of that meeting should be designed to give value to that prospect.

You should be going over the weaknesses and challenges of their current accounting function and showing them how they could strengthen those weaknesses.

You should be discussing their goals and describing what they would need in place to stand the best chance of achieving them.

You should be discovering the obstacles they face in achieving those goals and proposing how you can help them to overcome them.

This should be all about giving value and investing in the relationship BEFORE you even show them prices, proposals or terms of business.

In our firm, we request to see a set of their latest management accounts so we can start delivering that value straight away.

We assume they already are a client and aim to give the most value we possibly can.

This is not some sales ploy. You may only get these 40 minutes to impact this business in the best way you possibly can, and it's your ethical obligation to do so.

Tell them everything. Give away your secret recipe (not your secret sauce) but your secret recipe.

They won't be able to cook up the dish like you can. They will still need you. Knowledge is no longer valuable. It's your ability to deliver that knowledge through your service where the value exchange happens.

Jamie Oliver doesn't worry about someone setting up a restaurant next to his and putting him out of business just because he's given his recipes away in books, on YouTube, via his website and on TV.

The purpose of the systems that precede the Sales System – The Attraction System & Nurturing System – is to give value, invest into the client first and to share what you know through books, special reports, videos, webinars and live events.

This meeting is your golden opportunity to really ramp up the value and to use those 40 minutes to impact them as best you can; even if they go somewhere else with your recipe, even if they never work with you.

THE PRESENTATION

You should use a loosely structured visual presentation, which guides the meeting and gets over any key pieces of information you want them to know.

This presentation ensures consistency and again leverages accountants within your firm to fulfill the sales function of your business.

When I first met My Accountancy Place, they had ONE sales person (Paul) and FOUR accountants.

They now have FOUR sales people who are also accountants and don't forget, sales aren't restricted to new clients; they should also be being made to existing clients too.

In terms of presentation tools, I recommend Prezi™.

I use Prezi™ because it looks great, is in the cloud and it can be easily sent to the prospect afterwards. They can then deliver it again to their team and to other key decisions makers who they didn't turn up to the Proposal Meeting.

This becomes a powerful accompaniment to the proposal itself as your salesperson in the room.

If you have no presentation, or you have Powerpoint™ slides, stuffed with text talking about you, then you need to seriously address this as you will be unable to wow, give value or scale your operation beyond the key sales people in your company.

THE MEETING LOCATION

You have to make a judgment call as to where the Proposal Meeting should be held. It could be at your offices, at their offices, a neutral location or online.

I personally prefer for them to be held in our offices. This again puts you in control of the process, is a better use of your time and allows you to deliver an incredible experience, which blows their mind.

Once you have the system in place in your business, this frees you up to focus on the overall experience and permits you to do some really exciting things such as...

- Having their name and company logo printed on their parking space.
- Having a TV screen with their name and logo on as they arrive.
- Making sure that everyone in your team knows their name and greets them as they arrive.
- Having a cup with their name printed on it as a gift for them to take away, and for extra bonus points, you can have even found out what they like to drink and how they take it before hand (you can establish this in the Discovery Call.)
- Preparing the meeting space so it looks super professional.

Wherever you hold the meeting and whatever presentation tech you use, you've delivered value, answered their questions and now you're ready to provide them with the solution to overcoming their problems and reaching their goals...THE PROPOSAL

5. THE PROPOSAL

If the sales system that I've described here is the gateway that takes a prospect through to becoming a client, then the proposal itself is the keystone in that gateway.

I cannot stress the importance of this tool enough and the dramatic change in results in can produce if you get all the intricacies of it right.

What I am about to outline to you here has been a decade in the making, refining, honing and mastering.

And I promise to hold nothing back in sharing with you all that I've learnt about producing world-class proposals. Through this tool I will help you to sell more of your most profitable services, for higher fees and with an improved conversion rate.

And I'm also going to share with you the ultimate trick...how to do all of this with no effort, whilst you're sat with the client, so they could potentially sign up there and then.

We're talking grand master, voodoo, ninja proposal production here.

This changes EVERYTHING and sets you apart from nearly every other accountancy firm out there.

SPEED

So you know how it goes.

You've just completed a brilliant meeting and you promise the prospect that you'll have the proposal over to them by the end of the week.

Well that week turns into two and it eventually gets over to them, late and tagged onto an email filled with apologies and excuses.

Not only that...you hated doing it and the reason you hated doing it is because deep down, you know that it shouldn't be like this; that it could and should be so much easier.

This delay drags out the whole sales process and can create additional problems.

So the prospect leaves your meeting pumped and super psyched and ready to sign up. But between then and the proposal landing on their desk...anything can happen.

They could become distracted.

There could be a disaster at work.

Or worst of all...THEY TALK TO OTHER PEOPLE!!!

So if you've followed the rest of the guidance in this section, you should have presented them with a proposition that is significantly more than any other accountant they've seen so far, and definitely more expensive than the accountant they've just left.

If you give them the opportunity to TALK TO OTHER PEOPLE, they can easily be talked out of the solution you've just presented them with because the people they've talked to, were not privy to your conversation.

You MUST have the mechanisms to be able to produce a proposal INSTANTLY, whilst you're sat in front of the prospect.

You want to do this because...

- You don't want to waste time producing it later.
- You don't want to get in the way of them signing up.
- You don't want to allow anything to scupper your hard work.
- You want to start delivering value to their business straight away.
- You don't want to have to waste time and energy chasing them.
- You're not being fair to them if you make them wait.
- The process so far has turned them into a BUYER, so let them buy.
- You've probably told them during the proposal that you're going to save them time, so you don't want to start by wasting a moment, let alone a week or two.
- They EXPECT to be able to procure your services there and then, so at least meet their expectations.

The other BIG reason you want to produce the proposal straight away is because you want them to at least agree that this is the correct solution to their problems... WHILST they're still with you.

To send the proposal a week or so later is to rely on hope.

It's a fingers crossed approach.

To ping something over which they've NOT agreed to is asking for trouble because they'll either reject it straight away or you'll have to go backwards and forwards getting it agreed, and losing more of your precious time, which you don't have.

If they don't walk out of your meeting with a proposal then you've got this proposal meeting wrong.

But you can't even produce a proposal until you've agreed the services and fees, which are going to go into it.

MENU PRICING

Menu pricing is imperative if you are to build a scalable, thriving business.

You must have a clear menu of services whereby you can sit with the client and logically agree the services they need, how much that will cost and what the exact details of those services are.

This pricing menu needs to be used consistently across your entire team and all clients and done correctly, will inspire confidence in your prospect, because they will have greater belief in the pricing you're offering.

If they can't see exactly what services cost and they have a hint that these prices aren't set in stone, then they will begin to negotiate and won't be happy paying higher than expected prices.

Be clearly displaying your services and pricing, you will find that clients will buy more from you, will be happier to pay more and will sign up quicker.

This menu of pricing needs to be built on LOGIC, and not some emotional, sales psychology thinking, because accountants by their nature are logical people.

Also, it's important to understand that we're not selling here, we're closing the deal. Selling requires emotion and closing requires logic.

Everything up until this point should be emotional and exciting. We're now just into logic.

WHY 3 TIER PRICING DOESN'T WORK

I hear of a lot of accountancy firms offering their clients three tier pricing for their services. This doesn't work and is not fair on the client.

The success of their business is dependent on the finance function, which you provide. It's too risky to allow them to decide what they need.

If you were having an operation, you wouldn't want the surgeon asking you how many stitches you wanted. You would hope that they would put in the required amount to prevent you from dying.

It's the same with what services your client needs and the level of service they require.

You should have carried out your due diligence with that client to know where they are, where they want to get to and what they need to overcome to get there.

At this point there should only be one solution for them, if you are to be fair.

It's not for you to decide what they can afford

You need to present the right solution that prevents their business from dying.

The reason this normally doesn't happen is because the sales process hasn't been thorough, so you don't have the information you need and you don't have a menu of services. You it's normally a case of…"So what do you want?"

That should never be the case in your firm. It should always be a case of..."So based on what you've told me and in our expert opinion, this is what you need."

PRICING

So how should we price our I hear you ask?

This is the million-dollar question. Because if you fail to price your service profitably and consistently, then everything I've described in this book falls down.

What the point of making sales if they don't make you any money.

Being profitable is at the core of everything you do and I rarely meet an accountancy firm who knows how to price... even the big ones.

In our firm, we have this nailed.

It has taken years of refining but we have a very clear and fairly complex pricing methodology that ensures we don't leave any money on the table, we charge for everything and we don't permit scope creep.

We base our pricing on a range of factors such as their annual revenue, number of transactions, the quality of their record keeping, turnaround times and levels of support. But the trick is then to present that complexity as simply as possible to clients and your team.

This approach has allowed us to raise our minimum monthly fee to $650 at the time of writing this book and is helping to sign new clients and between $1000 - $3000 a month.

The other reason why you MUST to be profitable in the way that you price, is that you have to be a profitable firm. If you're not, what chance do you have of helping your clients to be profitable too, which is why they're coming to you in the first place.

Pricing and profitability is such a huge topic and beyond the scope of this book, but I have included a section at the end called "The 7 Pricing Strategies Of The Most Profitable Firms."

This will give you the firm foundations on which to start building your own pricing methodology.

PROPOSAL STRUCTURE

So a proposal is a proposal right?

Wrong.

Your proposal is a salesperson that goes back with the client after the meeting is over.

The structure of the proposal is critical if it is to convert the prospect with speed, with ease and with the option to upgrade to a better level of service that could deliver even greater value.

Let me take you through the proposal structure I've successfully used over the last ten years. I've used this structure across a wide range of businesses, but when I introduced it to the accounting industry, it was like it had been designed just for them.

I will quickly outline the structure of the winning proposal and then at the end of this section I will direct you to a place where you can produce an instant proposal for yourself, which you can start using straight away in your business.

1. **Front Cover** – Include a large, high quality version of your logo and the company name of the client you've produced this proposal for. They love reading their own name. Then include all the contact details of who produced the proposal and who the proposal is for. This helps both parties to get in touch with the other when they need to... fast!

2. **Contents Page** – They need to be able to see at a glance what the proposal contains and where to find what is most important to them…which is normally the costs.

3. **Introduction** – You need to explain what this proposal is all about and congratulate them for taking a step closer towards improving the accounting and finance function of their business. This doesn't need to be that long. They want to know what this is going to cost. But you need to make a promise as to how their future will be better if they take this step.

4. **Testimonial** – You want to follow up that introduction with a testimonial. The testimonial needs to support the promise you've just made them. If your service helps your clients to make better decisions about the future, your testimonial needs to describe how you've helped that specific client to make better decisions about their future. Keep it short and benefit focused. No-one really cares how nice you are, just that you have the ability to impact their business.

5. **Fees** – You need to provide a crystal clear list of the services they've opted for and what each of those services costs. You could just give an overall package price but there may be people in their business that want to see a breakdown of costs. This should be super clear and super smart. You are an accountant after all. The way you present the numbers is one of the most important parts of this proposal. A lot of firms hide this section near

the back of the proposal, thinking that the client will read everything you've put before it. They won't. Think about it. What would YOU do? You just want to see the costs right? So you need to present them early on, and provide the supporting evidence afterwards. I like to call them Investment Costs by the way...because this is an investment.

6. **Goal** – You want to remind them of the reason why they wanted your services in the first place. You need to inspire them to take the action you want. They've just seen your costs. This is going to hurt a little. It needs to. You now need to remind them of the greater pain they're going to overcome to get them past the pain of paying your higher monthly fee. So it goes...this is how much it's going to cost... and this is WHY!!!

7. **Next Steps** – You need to make it clear as to what they need to do next. They need to see it step by step and those steps need to be simple and pain free. You need to demonstrate how easy it's going to be to sign up for your services and to move their entire finance function over to you. It's easy, all you have to do is THIS!!! This is your call to action. It's what will bring in the money and so few firms have it in their proposal. Make sure it's in yours.

8. **Services Explained** – You now need to give a breakdown of the services they have chosen and the benefits those services will bring. It's also where you need to clearly outline the specific parameters of the services they've chosen. So if they've chosen Payroll, how many staff is it

for and frequently will it be done? If it's bookkeeping, how many transactions are you agreeing to reconciling for them each month and how often?

9. **Additional Services To Consider** – You also want to build in upsells into your proposal. You don't want a full list of everything you provide, but you do want to provide them with the next steps they'd need to take to upgrade their level of service with you. Most firms either show nothing or everything. You just need to show the next thing they will need from you and to lay it out on the roadmap ahead. They will need to know the cost of these additional services so they can make a decision to include them or not.

10. **Final Testimonial/Quote** – You now want to sign off the whole proposal with an inspirational quote or testimonial that is going to inspire action. Einstein, Tony Robbins or Bruce Lee all make great closing quotes that can inspire the action you want them to take i.e. sign-up.

"Insanity is doing the same thing and expecting different results"

– Einstein

"If all you ever do, is all you've ever done, then all you'll ever get, is all you've ever had."

– Tony Robbins

"Knowledge is not enough, we must try. Willing is not enough we must do."

– Bruce Lee

QUALITY

If the quality of your service is world class, then the quality of your proposal has to be world class too. In fact, every aspect of your service needs to be world class.

Imagine if you'd walked into a top class restaurant where you'd heard they served amazing food, and when you walked in, you were greeted with a miserable Maître D' as you walked in. What would you think?

I KNOW what you'd think...the same as me.

But if you changed that experience and made sure that your first impression was an amazing one, I know what would happen. You'd have a better time, spend more money, stay longer and tell more people about it. This is not complicated, so why should it be any different for accountancy firms?

It isn't.

Every aspect of your service needs to wow...especially your proposal.

If you want a client to spend $1,000 a month with you, then that's $12,000 a year. Over ten years that's $120,000.

If you want to be securing clients who are willing to pay you $120,000, then you have to provide a $120,000 experience as soon as they interact with you and then every step along the way.

ONLINE

The technology you use to produce your proposal needs to be online, not just on your computer.

You're a cloud accountant right? You know the benefits of the cloud so I shouldn't have to sell it to you.

But just in case you need a reminder...

- Any member of your team can access it, at any time.
- It can be utilised on a computer, but also on an iPad.
- It's safer and more secure.
- When you update it in one place, it is instantly updated everywhere else too.
- You live and die by the cloud...therefore live by it. To talk to your new prospect about the wonderful technology of Xero™ or QuickBooks™ and Receipt Bank™ and then to dive straight into Excel to generate a price just doesn't stack up.

AGREE THE FOLLOW UP

I learnt this very early on when I set up my first business.

Agree when you should follow up with the proposal. What most of us do is give someone a proposal and NOT agree when they should follow up.

You should aim to agree it in the proposal meeting.

A script I learnt early on is this...

"So how long do you think you'll need to be able to make a decision about this?"

Then whatever they tell you, challenge it by saying...

"Is that realistic? Will that give you enough time to speak to everyone you need to speak to, in order to make a decision?"

The reason you need to challenge them on the date is because you don't want to be badgering them when they're not in a position to make a decision. That will only annoy them.

Agree how long they need and then confirm a time and date.

Then here's the pincer move:

Get it booked into both of your diaries there and then.

You can even send them an invite.

Lock it down.

This is not being pushy. This is getting you in a position to be able to deliver the value you've promised, because until you get them to sign on the dotted line, no value has exchanged.

If you're not prepared to put in this level of effort to get them to sign up for your services, then I'm going to say you're not being fair to them, in fact, you're being selfish.

If you believe that you can genuinely deliver the value you're promising, positively impact their business, save them tax, save them time, improve their profits and genuinely change their lives for the better, then NOT to put in the effort to get them to sign is to be unfair to them.

It's unfair because they're either going to go without your services OR they're going to get them from someone else who won't be as good as you.

It is your ethical obligation to sell them the services they need in the quality and quantities you have proposed and to get them to sign up.

It's that simple.

But there IS a specific way to follow up that is not pushy and continues to give value.

6. THE FOLLOW UP

The follow up is where most businesses lose and ESPECIALLY accountancy firms.

The reason being is that...

- It takes time
- No-one has ever shown you how to follow-up properly
- The client's expectations haven't been properly managed
- We don't know how long to do it for
- We don't know what messages to communicate

So follow-up is key, and there are some distinct phases to the follow up process, which I've honed over the years of working with hundreds of businesses and helping them to implement this system.

AUTOMATION

Firstly, it's important to recognise that this process can be automated. This means you can create it once and it will run forever more.

Depending on which system you use, would determine how 'automated' it Is. Something like Mailchimp™ would allow you to create a series of follow up emails for example, which run on set days and for a specific period of time.

The business automation software that we use in our firm is Infusionsoft™.

Infusionsoft™ allows you to automate emails, texts, letters, trigger off Facebook ads, which coincide with your message and trigger off tasks for your Client Coordinators and Accountants to call the prospect.

If done properly, the messages can appear very personalised and the whole process will run on autopilot until a specific action happens, such as they signup or either they or you end the process. We don't need to get into details about this here, but just know that it can all be automated very simply.

If you'd like a map of our sales process, which we have in place with Infusionsoft™, visit JamesAshford.com/map and you can see it there.

IMMEDIATE FOLLOW UP

There are several distinct phases to the follow up process, which you need to stick to so that have the best chance of influencing the actions that you want and so that you don't annoy anyone.

The phase between the proposal meeting and the agreed follow-up date should be fairly light.

It's to be assumed at this point that they're moving forwards with the proposal and we don't want to appear too pushy or desperate, so we're going to be positive and leave them with space.

The first email should be sent during the Proposal Meeting itself and should contain the Proposal and Letter of Engagement. This means that they are armed with everything they need to proceed. This should describe the next steps and have a very clear CALL TO

ACTION. This should be driving them back to a page where they can digitally sign-off and accept your proposal. This email should also confirm the follow up date, which you agreed during the Proposal Meeting.

GEM ALERT

Can you remember me warning you about spotting the gems throughout this book? Well just in case you forgot that, I'm about to share one with you here that we've had tremendous success with.

As previously mentioned, we have automated emails throughout this system with automated videos that also get shared. But this step is a manual one that is a total slam-dunk, drop the mic, deal-making, game-changing move.

Videos are an incredible way to communicate with existing and potential clients. They deliver real wow and a great way to transfer massive value. As soon as the proposal is over, I would get your accountant who delivered the meeting to produce an instant, personalised video. We would simply do this as a screen capture video on our computer.

We would open up the proposal we've just produced for them and talk them through the services they've chosen and why we feel they will benefit them.

The reason for doing this is because they will no doubt forget certain things you told them and will likely be showing it to other people who weren't privy to your conversation.

On top of that, it genuinely wows them.

In this video, the script goes something like:

Hey James, it was great to have met with you today and thank you for inviting us to describe how we can positively impact your business moving forwards.

As discussed, we have a lot of experience of working with businesses like your own, helping them to overcome the challenges you're facing and in reaching the goals you've set for yourself.

[It's at this point where you run through the specifics of their proposal.]

If you or any members of your team have any questions at all, then please call me direct.

And if you would like to get everything started so that we can begin having the positive impact on your business, which we discussed, then just click the ACCEPT MY PROPOSAL button in the email I sent you and we'll get the boll rolling and making moving over to us as smooth as is possible.

Again, any questions, please get in touch and I look forward to working with you in the near future.

All the best...

You then take that video, upload it to YouTube or Vimeo, make it unlisted or private, embed it on your website and password protect it. You then send an email over to the client with a link to that web page to watch this video. This is the next-level activity I described at the beginning of this book.

Which other accountants are doing this? Hardly any, but this is the new world.

The final critical email that is a must, is the reminder email about the follow up call. This email should go out on the day before the call and should outline its purpose.

Keep it very conversational and make it clear that you'll be calling them to answer any questions they may have about moving forwards with the proposal, and to see if they're ready to make a decision.

That's it.

It should also contain another link for them to sign up so they are armed with everything they need to confirm acceptance of the proposal.

Done properly, they will have already done it BEFORE the call.

Now if this phase is a week or less, there is no need for any other correspondence unless specifically requested. But if it's over a week, I would certainly have another touch point.

This is designed to keep their interest in signing up and to reinforce the benefits of doing so.

One of THE most powerful ways of doing this would be in the form of an email with a video. This video should come from your firm's Key Person (so long as they're not incredibly boring) and should briefly reinforce the key benefits of moving forwards with the proposal. By brief, I mean like 60 seconds.

It should then transition into a short case study with an existing client, confirming how you have delivered those same benefits to them.

In the case study video, you could also ask your client this set of questions which are so powerful in helping to convert prospects into clients. These questions are:

1. What was life like before we started working with you and how did that make you feel?
2. How have we benefitted your business and how do you feel now?
3. What would you say to someone who had been given a proposal from us and were considering signing up for our services?
4. What would you like to thank us for?

Can you see how powerful those questions are?

Can you see how the answers to those questions would perfectly help transition that prospect from where they are now, to taking that next step with you?

And this video doesn't have to be fancy. Your iPhone with a decent microphone (I use the Rode Lapel mic) would be perfect.

You are then going to jump onto the call with this prospect, answer their questions and attempt to get them to hit that sign up button whilst you're on the phone, so you can crack straight on with the onboarding them

But if that doesn't happen, then we need to understand why that hasn't happened so we can determine what to do next?

A. Do they need longer to think about it? If so, no problem, how long?

B. Do they have any specific objections about moving forwards? If so, what are they?

C. Do they need to speak with other people? If so, who, and would they like you to be present too?

D. Have they decided to not proceed with yourselves at this time? If so, why, and is there anything that you could do to help change their mind, such as connect them up with a current client?

E. Is it just a definite no? If so, why? Where have we failed to communicate the value of moving over to us?

SHORT TERM FOLLOW UP

This relates to the As, Bs & Cs.

If they're still interested, but not ready to push the button just yet, we now need to keep in constant contact with them.

If you don't continue to help them to make the right decision, then again, you're not being fair to them. Just keep helping them to take baby steps forward.

On the call, make sure that you tell them you have a couple of emails that you'll be sharing with them that they will be able to take some real value from, whichever direction they choose to take.

This gives them an opportunity to say no, don't send me any more.

But DON'T apologise for these emails. They genuinely are designed to continue to give value.

They are a gift.

You now want to create three emails, preferably with videos (I love videos), that will be going out on the day after the call and then one a week for the next two weeks.

Now these emails have a definite change in tact.

Whereas up to this point we have been selling the benefits, they now know what they are and that's NOT why they haven't signed up yet.

The reason they haven't signed up is because they have reservations about moving forwards with you. They have objections, which you haven't uncovered yet.

In fact, they don't trust themselves to make the right decision and so we need to help them to build that trust and beneath whatever objection they tell you (you're too much, they like their current accountant, the hassle of changing systems would be too great etc.), there's always one, underlying objection that overrides them all - they don't want to make the same mistake again.

They will have made countless wrong decisions in their business and their life so far. You need to convince them that this isn't another one.

You need to convince them that the pain of staying where they are or choosing someone else or just doing nothing, is far greater than any pain of signing up with you, paying your higher fees, making the move or losing the 'friendship' (yeah right) of their old accountant.

People only make decisions based around two factors, which are to AVOID PAIN and to SEEK PLEASURE, and the former is the greater of the two motivators.

What we must do now, is to transition into dealing with objections. Don't hide behind them. Don't shy away from them. In fact...do the opposite.

Call them out first. Deal with them head on.

The three subject lines you may choose to have in the forthcoming emails could be...

    A.   Your Fees Are A Lot Higher
    B.   Moving Over To Xero/QuickBooks Will Be A Nightmare
    C.   My Old Accountant Has Been My Friend For Years

Then each of those emails tackle those objections and lead into specific examples of existing clients who had those exact thoughts, and how their businesses are different now they're working with you.

Again, I would get video testimonials to support this, and the best way to do that is to ask existing clients (who did have those objections) these questions...

1. What was life like before we started working with you and how did that make you feel?
2. How have we benefitted your business and how do you feel now?
3. What were your reservations about signing up for us initially?
4. What would you say to someone else who has those objections?
5. What would you like to thank us for?

Can you see what we're doing here?

Ideally I would like to get these two people to have a coffee together and for the client to convince the prospect to sign up. There's nothing more powerful than that. However this can be difficult to arrange (although not impossible if it's worth it.)

So the next best thing is to recreate that scenario though video and to ask the client the questions, that the prospect needs answering.

Most testimonial videos look pretty but are completely useless because the questions they were asked were irrelevant. No one ever thought how the video would be used strategically as part of a sales system.

I would much rather see a video filmed on you phone that's a bit ropey, but which tackles the questions that needs answering, over a highly produced video that's a waste of everyone's time and money.

Let's keep it real here.

You then need to follow this flurry of emails up with a call to see where they are. But let's say after that, they still don't go ahead and they need even longer to think about it or they're just not ready to proceed at this stage. Then what? Do we just forget about them?

No. We NEVER forget about them

I first learnt this lesson with a client I worked with who remained in contact with a prospect for TEN YEARS!!! TEN FREAKING YEARS!!!

Was it worth it? Well when they finally secured the contract, it was worth £5m, which, for a £12m turnover business was huge.

They then turned that £5m contract into a £10m contract over the next two years and then sold their business.

We had a client who we diligently followed up with for 12 months and when they signed, they were a £1,500 a month client. That's a lifetime value of £180,000.

So the answer is YES.

We NEVER stop following up.

But how should you follow up???

The same we follow up with D & E prospects.

LONG TERM FOLLOW UP

So this is how we follow up with those clients who haven't made a decision yet, including Ds and Es.

We are now in a position where these prospects have not chosen to proceed with us…YET!

Now most accountants would let these prospects go at this stage but this is a huge waste. We've not got them this far for it to stop here, so don't let them go.

So what do we know about them? Two things…

1. The haven't told us to never darken their door again
2. We know when their year end is

So what we do at this point is to enter them into a long-term nurture process. This is where we email and post useful reports to them every fortnight or at the very least, every month… FOREVER!!!

This normally frightens accountancy firms because you've been sent loads of pushy correspondence in the past, which you found annoying, and you don't want to be that guy.

But there's a different approach.

CONTINUE TO INVEST

In this approach, we continue to invest in the relationship; we continue to help and to give value.

Just because they haven't chosen to work with you yet, doesn't mean to say that you can't still help them and if this is automated, it takes no effort (other than the initial setup) for it to run forever more.

Therefore, could you produce 12 articles, 12 videos, 12 case studies or 12 short reports that could benefit a prospect? Of course you could; or your team certainly could.

If you could do that, then you could easily build a 12-month nurturing sequence. As well as this, you could post gifts to them. I love sending books to prospects as it really shows that you connect with their way of thinking. Spending £50 on books throughout the year is well worth it to land a £500/month client who stays with you for the next ten years.

Another great thing to do would be to invite them to events. In our firm we have a Round Table event for our clients which we run every month, where we bring in guest speakers to inspire and help our attendees. What we also cleverly do is invite potential prospects to those events too.

We are constantly investing in the relationship and giving value BEFORE we even get the business.

So that's the first thing…Invest.

The second thing is that as we get closer to their year-end (which we learnt during the Discovery Call) we begin to ramp things up.

In month ten of their year for example, you could be sending them advice about how they could minimise the tax they pay for the following year.

Because you have now given them so much value, you are now in a fair enough position to ask them straight out if they'd like to have another conversation about working together.

You have invested in them. They can see that you deliver on your promise, so now just ask them...

"Hi, hope you're well and that you've had a prosperous year.

I know we had a conversation last year and I just wondered if now was the right time for us to have another discussion about how we can provide the accounting and finance function of your business.

Unless I hear differently, I'll give you a bell in a few days time to see if this is something you'd like to explore again.

It will also just be great to catch up and find out how things are progressing."

You can now follow this up with a phone call and any additional emails if need be.

There is nothing stopping you from repeating this process year in, year out and it can all be automated.

The key principle I'm employing here, is one which underpins all of my systems which is...SEAL THE CRACKS.

Before you spend any money in attracting any more prospects or having any more meetings with them, you must first seal the cracks in the process that follows. Without developing this system, you will no doubt be wasting money and time, burning through a list of prospects that may one day choose to work with you. Be fair to these prospects and install the system that invests in them first and gives them the best chance of signing up for your outstanding service.

Throughout all of this automation, you can be calling them, inviting them for lunch, inviting them to your webinar, passing them referrals, finding out how they're getting on...anything!!!

You just need to be front of mind and as soon as they're ready to press the button, you're the first firm they think of.

If you think this is too much, you will lose out to the firm who doesn't.

This works because it works for us.

Play the long game.

Continue to invest.

7. THE SIGN UP

So here we are, the big moment...the sign up.

This is where they go from prospect to client in one swift move. The important aspect of this stage is to make it easy and to remove any obstacles.

This process ideally needs to:

- Be online so it can be signed anywhere and anytime
- Be instantly available as soon as the proposal is created because they may want to proceed there and then.
- Capable of completion within 60 seconds
- Be legally compliant with their ACTUAL signature and a check box that acknowledges that they've read, understood and have agreed with your terms.
- Instantly trigger off the next system in the process, which is the Onboarding System. This is where you can really wow them.
- Instantly trigger off the invoicing and payment collection.
- Send them a signed copy of their Letter of Engagement as proof of their signup.

When I first implemented this system with our firm and automated this exact process, the owner – Paul - stepped back and watched his senior accountants deliver the presentation to businesses that were as big as he had ever signed up himself and they signed up within days. This was one of the most exciting and encouraging stages in our time working together because he had 4 people at this level, now all ready to sign up this big clients (true story.)

So this aspect of the system should be relatively easy to implement, but the place where you win and totally OWN this system is in the transition to the next step.

THE NEXT STEP
So picture this...

1. Your proposal was produced instantly and sent to the client with a link to the Letter of Engagement.
2. They clicked the link and digitally signed the LoE within seconds.
3. They then received an instant, signed copy of this in their inbox as well as being instantly directed to a web page on your website
4. On this web page they saw a video of you, welcoming them to your accountancy firm and congratulating them for making such a great decision.
5. You then tell them that in order to move things forward, all we need to do, is to capture some basic information, but don't worry if you don't have everything to hand, just tell us what you know.
6. Then immediately below this video, there was a form for them to fill out (while they're all excited about signing up for your service.)

7. At the end of completing that form, they are then asked to complete the direct debit mandate, to make payment collection super easy.

8. MEANWHILE...Your Client Coordinator has been sent an instant message to call this new client to welcome them to your business and to tell them what happens next.

9. Also, the invoicing was triggered in your accountancy software, which will now be sent out automatically.

10. Ideally, workflows would have been triggered to start onboarding that client and delivering your service to them.

So they've signed-up, been welcomed virtually, given you all the information you need to successfully onboard them, been invoiced, set up their payment to you, been welcomed in person and wheels have begun to turn to onboard and service that client.

This is the world-class level I'm talking about.

The great news for you is that there is technology that is within easy reach that can allow you to operate at this level, with next to no effort, once it has been properly setup. A lot of accountants attempt to install systems like this, but it ends up crumbling and so they blame the technology. The problem is rarely with technology and nearly always with the process in the first place. If the process is sound, solid, crack-free and proven, then it can be run with a pen, paper, and checklist.

The magic isn't in the technology - the magic is in the process.

IMPLEMENT THE SYSTEM

Ok, so by now you should be fired up and excited about implementing some or all of this system. However, with that also comes an element of overwhelm.

It's like getting to the top of what you think is the mountain, only to look up and realize you've only got to basecamp and Everest is in front you. The key to implementing this system is in just getting started. It's in progress not perfection.

What ONE thing could you take from this today and implement?

Is it a video you do on your iPhone?

Is it in a follow up email you write?

Is it in sharing this book with the rest of your team?

Is it in holding a meeting with them to share some of the key principles?

Is it in stopping doing something you currently do which you now perceive as damaging?

But in order to get motivated with this, you must first move.

The word motivation coms from the Latin – motivus, which mean 'to move'. You've just got to start.

As a wise man once said, you don't have to be great to start, but you have to start to be great.

Don't worry about things being average when you first put them out there, you must pass through average to get to great. Don't worry about everything being perfect. Just start and fix it as you go.

What I've done here is to lay out the blueprint. You just need to start implementing it today whilst you're fired up about it; whilst you're in the mindset. Just do what you can with what you have, but the key word here is DO. Otherwise, this will have been just another book that was good to read, but that has had NO impact in your life at all.

But before you start going out there making more sales and serving your clients to a higher level, you must fist ensure that what you're selling is going to make you money.

If the way that you price your services means that you are not very profitable, then as you sell more, you are creating more problems for yourself.

So before one more sale happens, let's make sure that what you're actually selling is profitable for you.

BE MORE PROFITABLE

If you're not as profitable as you could be, then you must correct this before you make one more sale. Otherwise, you're filling a leaking bucket. This is a waste of your time, your energy and a waste of potential profits, which you could be easily making. Sealing those holes must be your number one priority.

As an accountancy firm, your clients expect and want you to be highly profitable. Because if you're not, what chance do you have of helping them to be profitable? And that's one of the main reasons they came to you.

So let me show you how to seal the holes and maximise your profits.

MODEL WHAT WORKS

Presumably, you're reading this book now because you've hit some sort of breaking point.

There's something you're trying to get past and you're looking for answers. This might be that you want to make more money, make more profit, or have more time or give more value. But whatever it is, you're feeling overwhelmed and frustrated. You're frustrated because you know you could do more, achieve more and that life could and should be simpler. If that's the case, you can either:

- Breakdown
- Breakaway
- Breakthrough

Accountants have breakdowns. Fact. It's not ideal but it can sometimes be the catalyst that brings about the change they so desperately need. However, we'll try to avoid this option if at all possible.

Accountants also breakaway from their practice and go into industry. I'm sure you've even got your calculator out in those dark moments to look at what you COULD be earning without all the stress. But you probably dismissed that fairly quickly as you realised you're unemployable, and that's probably a good move too.

So you're the one who wants to breakthrough. Am I right?

If so, you fall into one of two camps.

CAMP ONE – The stubborn accountant who doesn't need any help and who will figure it out if it's the last thing they ever do. This is the person who refuses to ask for help when they can't find the thing they're looking for in a large store. They'd rather waste hours of their life to find that 'thing' rather than ask someone who knows exactly where it is, and would probably get it for you if you slipped them a couple of quid. This person will eventually breakthrough, but only with a struggle and over a period of time, which could be years. Yes it saves you money and your pride, but the costs can be huge.

CAMP TWO – The smart accountant who finds someone who's achieving the results they want to achieve and they copy them. That's it. It may cost you money, but the savings are in time, energy and stress.

I meet both. I also meet numbers 'ones' who I give the answers too, but who insist on ripping them up and insist on creating their own map to success only for them to return at some point in the future, to say OK, I've tried it my way, I got lost, let me start again with your map (and I promise not to rip it up this time.) Number one becomes number two and that's fine.

So the bottom line here is, just model what works. Find the accountancy firms who are profitable, growing and who already have watertight pricing systems and steal theirs. Life is short. Move on to solving the next problem.

"Good artists copy, great artists steal." - Pablo Picasso

CHARGE PER TRANSACTION

If you are still charging by the hour, then you are punishing yourself for being good and preventing yourself from growing. Allow me to elaborate:

The thing your client values above all things is time; theirs and not yours.

Your client only cares that you can deliver value, impact their business, help them to make better decisions about the future and save them time.

If you could reconcile their accounts and send them their management accounts report three days after month end, is that more valuable or less valuable than another accountancy firm who takes three weeks to complete the same task? (Assuming that the value of the information was the same.) If time was valued, then your answer would be three weeks.

But your answer wasn't three weeks. It was three days.

So you value speed over time, because you know that if your client can receive something faster, then they can make better decisions about the future, which will save them money and shorten the time it takes for them to become more successful.

So why are you still charging around time?

If you charge based on time, then there is no incentive for you to improve efficiencies with better technology, better systems, better staff or outsourcing. So you therefore restrict your own growth and create a lose-lose situation between you and your client.

What we use at My Accountancy Place and what I teach in the firms I work with is to productise your services and to charge around transactions rather than time.

So let's take bookkeeping as an example.

If you charge me an amount for the time it takes you to reconcile my accounts each month, then you've nailed your firm to the floor.

We charge £1 per transaction that we reconcile and we have bandings and charge to the upper amount in the band.

So for example...

- 0 – 49 transactions
- 50 – 74 transactions
- 75 – 99 transactions
- 100 – 124 transactions

Therefore, if you have an average of 85 transactions per month, you would fall into our 75 – 99 transactions band and would be charged £1 x 99 = £99 per month.

We then multiply this by the frequency of reconciliation. If you don't have this factor in there, it's very easy to lose control of the client and of your profits.

So we also charge by:

- Monthly reconciliation x 1
- Weekly reconciliation x 1.5
- Daily reconciliation x 2

If you have an average of 85 transactions per month that you'd like reconciled weekly, you would be charged £1 x 99 x 1.5 = £149 per month.

You see with this method, there's no emotion involved. We're just using logic to assess the fee because we've spent years refining it and working closely with some other profitable firms to make sure we're all on point.

How does this sit with you? Does it make sense or could you see possible challenges from clients or your staff? If so, don't worry, you're not the first.

But you know what?

This is your business. So, your game. Your rules.

Once you've established them, I promise you, life will become so much simpler for you and the overwhelming feeling will start to go. There are ways to navigate through this period of change, and it's not as difficult as you may think.

DO QUARTERLY FEE REVIEWS

So this neatly brings us into fee reviews and two questions...

- How often do you do them?
- How do you do them?

You see, the greatest potential you have for growth right now rests with your existing clients and unless you're carrying out regular fee reviews, and by regular I mean quarterly AND you're doing them in the right way, then I know you're leaving money on the table, allowing profits to trickle through your fingers and not serving your clients to the extent that you could be.

So let's start with 'how often?'

The reason you need to be carrying out fee reviews quarterly is because your client's circumstances change. They take on more staff. They have more bank transactions. They have more challenges, which need to be overcome. They set new goals, which need to be reached.

If you're not constantly adjusting the level of service you're providing, then you are being unfair to your clients because you won't be providing them with all the value they need.

So this brings us to HOW you do them, because this has nothing to do with fees. If you're focusing on fees, then it's all about you, when it's not. It's all about the client.

Your fee reviews should be based around 5 key areas. We remember them by actually renaming the process as GLOSS Reviews™. This stands for:

Goals – where are they heading?

Location – where are they now?

Obstacles – what's holding them up?

Speed – how fast do they want to go?

Services – what services do they need from us to reach their goals and overcome their obstacles at the speed they want to go, based on their current circumstances?

When we introduce this concept to clients, they typically increase their GRF (Gross Recurring Fee) by 20% within 3 months.

Now I know what's going through your head...

How the hell are we going to carry out fee reviews every three months? We're struggling to do it every three years!?!?!?!? If this is what you're thinking, then you're no different than every other firm out there.

At My Accountancy Place, we attempted to solve this problem by using the best technology we could find. We were using the leading software on the market at the time, but the challenges we faced were:

- The process was clunky.
- We weren't able to price in the way we wanted to.
- Generating letters of engagement had a manual element to their production.
- We had to get existing clients to sign new letters of engagement off which slowed the process down.
- It wasn't clear to clients and wasn't very compelling as a sales tool.
- Not all of our team used it.
- The whole thing took too long to complete and so it didn't get used as often as it should have.
- It looked like we had a system but we didn't. We had chaos.

You see, all of these products were designed in a slower world. In a world where people couldn't order an item off Amazon and have it delivered within an hour. In a world where you couldn't order your children's school uniform at 9pm at night and for them to be wearing it to school in the morning. The world is now a very different place.

Your clients are too knowledgeable and too powerful to put up with anything less than world class.

We needed a system that:

- All of our accountants used.
- Wowed our clients.
- Simplified the whole process.

- Could go from agreeing fees, to signing the client up AND generating the invoice to take payment off them... IN LESS THAN THREE MINUTES i.e. whilst we were still sat with the client.

We concluded that if the system couldn't do that, then our team would never use it, and we'd never be able to hit our target of quarterly fee reviews.

In the end, we bit the bullet, hired in some of the best developers and designers from the UK & Australia and we developed our own systems that perfectly met the requirements of a fast growing, cloud-based, entrepreneurial thinking firm of accountants. Yes it cost us the price of a house to build and a LOT of refining to perfect it, but the growth this has now enabled us now and in the future has been immense.

In the first 9 months of using the tool we developed, we grew our GRF by 50%. Which on a half a million pound revenue firm was impressive and naturally attracted the attention of other firms who wanted to know: 'how?'

We appropriately called it **The 3 Minute Proposal Tool**.

CHARGE FOR EVERYTHING

Our average monthly fee is just over £450 a month, but we also have clients paying us £1000 and £2000+ a month.

Now this isn't down to the fact that we're particularly more expensive than other accountancy firms, we just charge for everything!!!

You know if you go and buy a Mercedes car, and you want a push start button instead of a key, you'll pay extra for it.

You know if you want 21" alloys instead of the 19", you'll pay extra for it.

They won't give you one thing extra without charging you for it, because in doing so, they devalue the price of every other Mercedes on the road.

Think about it in other scenarios, restaurants for example.

If you go to a restaurant and want a side order of something, you pay extra for it. And rightly so.

So why should it be any different in the way that you charge and sell your services.

TIME

Now we only believe in a **recurring monthly model,** so if someone's calling us up and wanting our time each month, we'll take the hit in the first instance, but then after that, we will add either a Support Package, or a Mentoring Package or a Board Level Package to their recurring monthly fee.

This will enable them to access a limited amount of our time, from a certain level of staff, access to a limited number of SOS calls and access to certain online training.

We don't want to hit them with surprise bills where possible. We'd rather agree a higher level of support and crack on.

ANNUAL ACCOUNTS

If we're pricing your Annual Accounts, then we take into consideration the quality of your record keeping.

For excellent records we decrease the fee by 30% and for terrible record keeping, we increase it by 50%, because we know there's more work to do.

We would also take into consideration your annual revenue because again, if you make more money, it's going to take us longer to account for it.

BOOKKEEPING

As I mentioned before, if they want their bank transactions reconciled weekly rather than monthly then that's fine, it just costs 50% more.

Charging for EVERYTHING is where you really seal the cracks in your pricing system and where you make it watertight.

But should I tell you where you will get massive value with this?!?!?!

Helping your clients to do the same.

Helping your clients to implement similar, watertight pricing principles into THEIR business is one of the fastest ways you can impact their revenue and profit, but most accountants miss out on it.

Do you know why? Because they're not doing it themselves.

How on earth can they help their clients to be more profitable if they're not first maximizing their own profits? The only way you can do that is to CHARGE FOR EVERYTHING!!!

GROW YOUR MONTHLY RECURRING REVENUE

I'm probably preaching to the converted here, and as I've already mentioned, you need to be growing your monthly recurring revenue, rather than hitting your clients with one-off bills throughout or at the end of the year.

This is the ONLY model for us for several very good reasons:

1. The client can manage their finances better. Rather than getting hit with a big bill at the end of the year, clients actually prefer to pay monthly because they know where they are with their finances.

2. You can manage your finances better. If you know what you have coming in every month, it allows you to make better decisions about how you should grow your own business.

3. It's easier to grow your revenue. As I outlined before, carrying out regular fee reviews allows you to easily add new services and charge more if your client's circumstances have changed. This is almost impossible to manage if you're charging annually. Charging monthly allows you to easily adjust their fee and crack on.

4. You don't have to chase the client for money. We use GoCardless which is connected to Xero via Directli. So all we have to do is amend their invoice in Xero and the new fee will be automatically taken the very next month. You might not have GoCardless in your country, but you can achieve similar results with Stripe or IntegraPay. Your monthly collection method needs to be nailed on.

5. You get paid faster. If you charge your client once you've completed their annual account and it takes you 8 months to complete them, you could be waiting 20 months before you get your cash. No good. You need to be getting paid from day one.

6. It removes surprising bills and hatred. If you're hitting your client with one-off bills throughout the year, know this...they hate you for it. At My Accountancy Place, let's say someone starts ringing up for advice or additional support throughout the month, rather than hit them with a one-off bill for it, we have a different tact. We'd take the hit on the first month and then in the following month say "Hey, it looks like you're needing additional support from us, so rather than hit you with large, one-off bills and discouraging you from calling us, we're going to put you on our SOS Support package. This gives you the confidence that you can pick up the phone anytime and talk to us and it's only £50 a month. How does that sound?" Now in the service schedule, we'd limit the liability of this support to 15 minutes max each month and it doesn't roll over. If the support goes over 15 minutes, we just increase the package to our next level.

7. You can incentivise your team to help you to grow. Again, your team is your greatest asset and leveraging them is the fastest way to grow. You can't grow your business, you can only grow your people, and they will grow your business for you. If you have recurring monthly fees, it's easy to incentivise your team. We pay-out half the monthly fees for the first month to the person who signs them up, as a bonus. If they are able to sell an additional service to a client, then we pay out half of that increase for the first month too. This is almost impossible to do if you're charging annually, because you'd be paying out money that you don't have.

8. You can set goals better. If you know your goal is to increase your monthly revenue by two grand a month, it's far easier for you to reach that goal. You can put clear plans in place to bring on new clients and that aren't based on the number of new clients, but rather the collective value of them. You can also set plans in place to grow an existing client's revenue by a certain amount too. Without this, it's difficult to set goals and therefore nearly impossible to set plans in place to reach them. Without this, you stay stuck where you are.

So, can you see how that small decision to take payments monthly rather than annually has such a huge knock on effect. Get it wrong and you create frustration throughout your firm and keep yourself rooted to the spot.

Get it right and you create win-win-wins for yourself, your clients and your team.

If you're currently not doing this and you're worried about how you should approach your clients, then just be honest and apologise. Just say something like "I'm sorry that we've been charging you annually. We know this is no good for your cash flow and so we're moving you over to monthly payments. This will allow you to plan your finances out better so you'll know exactly where you are each month. You're going to be paying us this way so you don't even have to worry about making the payment each month. So your new payments will start next month, and we're also going to carry out a GLOSS Review™ at the same time to ensure that we're serving you as best we can. So let's get a date booked in the diary to get this sorted."

If you're not doing it, just do it.

If you are doing it, do it better.

USE LOGIC NOT EMOTION

Accountants don't like selling. They don't even like salespeople.

Now YOU might, because you understand its importance in the survival and growth of your business, but what about the rest of your team?

The only way you can implement these profit maximising strategies is by leveraging your greatest asset - your team.

You can't do this yourself.

You just don't have time to figure out what every other profitable accountancy firm is charging. You don't have time to figure out the optimum pricing model to ensure no more leakage of profit, and you certainly don't have time to be carrying out fee reviews with regularity I'm suggesting here, that's not to mention the signing up of new clients.

What happens is that Accountancy Firm Owners, Directors and Partners go out and get systems and learn new strategies which excite them and get them pumped up, because this is the thing that's going to break them through.

Then they bring this new strategy or system in, and they rally the troops together and they hit them with this ground breaking, thought leading, life changing, value enhancing methodology and then...nothing.

Just blank faces stare back at you and inside they're scared to death at the thought of selling. I mean, come on, they're accountants...selling is beneath them right?

This is where you can have the best strategy in the world, but if the mind-set of everyone responsible for implementing that strategy is not in total alignment, then it fails.

So the reason why selling doesn't sit well with accountants is because selling is emotional and accountants are more logical beings.

So, if you want to leverage the greatest asset you have, and you want to back yourself out of the running of your business and start to really free yourself up to work strategically and to have the life that you want, then you need to have a LOGICAL PRICING SYSTEM.

One great approach to this is to outline the different stages your client's businesses go through in terms of revenue, number of employees and years in business, the problems they face at each phase and the service level a client of that size needs.

That way, it's very LOGICAL to explain that other clients of a similar size and at a similar stage in the growth cycle, tend to have these services from us. It just depends how much time you want to save and how fast you want to grow your business.

Again, we invested in having this model developed and it also outlines what level of investment they should be making into the finance function of their business at each phase. We call it our "Stages of Success" model.

This really helps our accountants to prescribe the correct service level to the client, using a consultative, logical sales process.

Also, because everything is accounted for in the way we price our services, if they don't like the price, we simply adjust the service level or take something out. There's no haggling or negotiating.

Waiters in restaurants don't haggle.

They simply hand you a menu and you choose what you want, where each dish assembles a collection of ingredients to delight a certain type of customer.

Why should it be any different in your accountancy firm?

Yes, it's hard to develop recipes and to create the menu, but it only needs creating ONCE. And this is far better than the alternative, which is EVERY SINGLE TIME.

If most accountancy firms dropped their accountants into this role, with the pricing model they have, they'd be forever saying "I'll just ask the chef to see if he can do that."

You're the Chef.

In fact you're the Head Chef.

You don't want to be cooking. You want to be developing recipes that wow your clients and then create a simple, logical menu that allows your team to easily present the value of your dishes to your clients.

If your current pricing system includes emotion, haggling, negotiation, ambiguity, 3 levels for this, 3 levels for that or a collection of ingredients for your clients to assemble and turn into dishes themselves, then you are in emotional turmoil.

If, on the other hand, you have assembled those ingredients into stunning dishes, which perfectly suit the palate of your ideal clients and you present them with clarity for your team to serve, then you'll win.

And if your clients are free to add side orders or easily take out certain ingredients as their palate and wallet allow, then isn't that a far simpler way to price and to sell?

Most accountants do one of two things.

They either invite the client to look in the fridge and say these are all the ingredients we have, what can I cook for you. Or they say we only sell fish and chips here, do you want it or not?

But you are not most accountants.

YOU are a 5-star Michelin chef.

PLAN OUT THE ROADMAP

There's a dangerous mind-set that accountants can have which is a 'them and us' approach to their clients.

The moment you start to see yourself as a business owner and not an accountant, is the moment you stand shoulder to shoulder with your clients and can start looking down the same road together. You don't need to be able to see the full length of the journey.

A car can cross the whole of America in the dark, by only lighting up the few hundred yards in front of the car.

You only need to be able to see a certain distance ahead, and then when we get there, we can adjust our course to stay on track towards our destination.

So using everything else I've shared with you here – leveraging your team, logic not emotion, charging for everything, quarterly fees reviews – we are now able to say to our clients OK, so this is what lies ahead on the road and this is what we can do to help you to reach your goals and overcome your obstacles faster.

You can then explain that once that goal is achieved, be it in three months or sixth months, then you're going to need this from us to get you the rest of the way.

There is a school of thought that says you should sell your clients as much as you can initially because it's difficult to get them to buy anything else off you in the future.

This is old school thinking, makes no sense and can be dangerous.

By working with the client in **partnership**, we find we're able to have a mature conversation about what they're going to need from us now and what they'll need from us next. People call this upselling. We call it up-serving.

TAKE MASSIVE ACTION

Statistics suggest that only 5% of people who attend conferences and seminars will actually do anything with what they learn and interestingly, that 5% would have done it anyway, whether they attended the conference or seminar or not.

The most profitable accountants are without doubt the ones who take action continually. They are motivated enough to take the initial actions required to get started, which builds the momentum to keep them going.

They are the ones who focus on progress and not perfection because if you wait for perfection, you'll never start.

They are the ones who start and fix things as they go, knowing that whatever they start with will be better than what they had last week, but not as good as what they will have next week.

In Japanese business, there is an award, which is fiercely competed for every year called the Deming Prize. It's awarded to the company who displays the greatest degree of Kaizen.

Kaizen translates as continual and never-ending improvement.

The philosophy of Kaizen is that if something keeps improving, then over time the results compound and lead to exponential growth. And it was this philosophy that saw war-torn Japanese businesses with no electricity and no running water emerge as some of the most successful businesses in the world.

There will be accountants who read this and for whom nothing will change. They will take these ideas into meetings and out of them again. These accountants will stay stuck where they are while others pass them by and they'll continue to be frustrated by their bottom clients and failing to fully serve their top clients.

There will also be other accountants who just start. They will take action. They will take these strategies and implement them in their next fee review meeting or with their next prospect. They will make mistakes. They may feel embarrassed. But it's only in taking those first steps that they will pass through into the thriving, profitable firm they know they could be. And it's these accountants who will serve their clients better, for longer, get paid more and have less frustration.

I believe that over the next 12 months we're going to see a massive divide in accountancy firms. Those who are thinking entrepreneurially, standing shoulder to shoulder with their clients, building profitable businesses themselves and driving forward at pace and those who are clinging on to the wreckage of compliance accounting, charging by the hour and fighting over the scraps of what cloud accounting has left them, for now.

Remember, you are not an accountant, you're a business owner.

But most accountants don't have a business, they have chaos.

And while you have chaos, you're unable to spend time on what's important and you'll forever be dragged into what's not important.

The chaos ends when you take control of your systems and the system that needs to be watertight and locked in first is your sales system and pricing methodology.

THE RED PILL

Have you ever seen the film 'The Matrix'?

If so, you'll know that Neo (Keanu Reeves) was offered the blue pill, to go back to how everything was before and forget everything he'd learned. Or the red pill, where he'd be given all the answers he'd been looking for in one hit.

The red pill in your case is **GoProposal™**.

After other accountancy firms found out about our **3 Minute Proposal Tool**, they wanted it and we were amazed at the quality of firms who wanted to get on board.

These were the thought leaders in accounting; the entrepreneurially thinking, profitable accountants. They came wanting our solution, but they also brought their own ideas about how it should work and their innovations around pricing. Together, we worked them into the system.

Hence, we further developed the 3 minute tool and created **GoProposal™**. Our goal was very clear – to create the best pricing and proposal tool for accountants in the world, that was easy to use and which used the most profitable accountants pricing models.

GoProposal™ has been recognised as the number one pricing and proposal system for accountancy firms who want to serve their clients better. And so in a book which talks about your ethical obligation to sell, it would be remiss of me not to now attempt to sell you on the one thing, which I believe could transform the fortunes of your firm, and help you to serve your clients to a higher level. The benefits of GoProposal™ include...

- It comes fully loaded with the services and pricing from our firm and some of the most profitable and successful accountants around, so you can instantly model all of their pricing methods.

- The pricing methods are watertight and prevent leakage of profit and control and allow you to layer the pricing up with complex calculations if need be.

- The system uses logic and not emotion to help leverage your entire team to use the system by providing total transparency for your team and your clients.

- It allows you to plan the roadmap ahead with your clients using our up-serving principles, easily showing them what they'll need next.

- It allows your team to agree on fees, automatically produce a proposal, auto-generate the letter of engagement, get clients to digitally sign it and to fire off the invoice in your accounting software and to take payment from your client...whilst you're sat with them.

- It is fully configurable to make it work and look exactly as you want it.

- You get to join our incredible online community to engage and ask questions.

- You get a 30-day free trial to prove the concept to yourself and your team.

- You will be able to get clients increasing fees by 2 times, 3 times and 4 times with little effort and no drama.

- You can package up your services AND we even give you a copy of our "Stages of Success" model to prescribe the correct service level to the client, using a consultative, logical sales process.

- You get access to our online training academy for you and your team to discover how to get the most out of this powerful system in practice.

But above ALL of this, GoProposal™ will help you to end the chaos. It will give you a truly watertight system that will help you to take complete control of your clients and your team. This is the start of you controlling the chaos and the foundation on which to build all other systems.

It can be easy to dismiss it, thinking you already having something 'similar' in place. I assure you, there is nothing similar to this. The philosophy on which it is built is different to everything else out there and it's so subtle, you'd be forgiven for missing it.

But the philosophy is aligned with standing shoulder to shoulder with your clients and maximising the lifetime value from them. It is aligned with accountancy firms who want to break free from the traps of charging for compliance work and who want to break through to having the greatest impact they possibly can with their clients.

GoProposal™ isn't a piece of technology or just a new system.

GoProposal™ is a methodology, a philosophy and a community.

If you're committed to ending the chaos, building a thriving business and impacting YOUR clients in the deepest, most meaningful and most profitable ways possible, then join us.

You are not an accountant. You're a business owner.

JOIN THE REVOLUTION

and start your free trial today at

GoProposal.com

WHAT OUR CLIENTS SAY

"In the four months we've been using GoProposal, it has allowed us to increase our annual revenue by an additional £100k. Half of which has come from new clients and the other half has come from existing clients. AND... I haven't produced a single proposal. My team now do them.

Paul Barnes | Founder of My Accountancy Place

"Our conversion rate has increased by 30% since using GoProposal. This is the best pricing product that we've seen on the market and has enabled us to maximise the value we provide to our clients."

Phil Ellerby | Founder of Northern Accountants

"I've just signed up a 1 director Ltd company for £626 +VAT per month, by far my largest every customer – not sure I would have ever priced in this way before. My largest before was probably around the £300 mark – so a massive difference, & it feels awesome."

Nick Kay | Founder of Pavilion Accountancy

"GoProposal is now the hub of my business. I have real comfort and confidence that this system is being driven by the right person who's a sales and systems expert, and not an accountant."

Martyn Hodgson | Founder of Swirral Accountancy

"The old ways don't work anymore and you need to fundamentally change. Using GoProposal we increased one client's fees from £2750 to £6250 and the way I see that is that he's now receiving over double the value from us."

Martin Wardle | Director at Robson Laidler

ABOUT THE AUTHOR

James Ashford works exclusively with leading firms of accountants from around the world, helping them to systemize their firms so they can deliver maximum value and incredible experiences to their clients.

James is the founder of GoProposal, bestselling author of "Selling to Serve" and Director at My Accountancy Place.

Graduating with a Masters Degree in Innovative Design, James was hailed by the Design Council of Great Britain as being one of the top most innovative people in the UK. His earlier experiences have included teaching in Art in prisons and being a close-up magician. It is through these experiences and working across a vast range of design disciplines that James found his real passion in helping & inspiring businesses and individuals to become the very best they can be.

Becoming passionate about psychology, marketing and business breakthrough strategies, James has worked with many leading businesses, helping them to implement robust systems using Infusionsoft. He has helped to increase profits whilst enabling the business owners to free up their time to create thriving company cultures.

James is constantly studying the world's greatest companies and individuals to discover how they've succeeded, which he melds with his passion and inspiration and shares with his client's and fans.

In recent years, James has taken his well-earned wealth of knowledge and is applying this specifically to the accounting industry. It is thought leading and inspiring many accountants around the world to maximize the value they're giving to their clients.

He authors a successful business blog and podcast via **www.JamesAshford.com**, which you can subscribe to for free and where he continually shares his best content.

He also continually publishes videos outlining the successes he achieves with the firms he is working with on LinkedIn, Twitter, Facebook and YouTube.

Just search those social networks for 'James Ashford', connect and say "Hi".

WHAT NEXT?

1. Sign up for your free trial of GoProposal™

2. Connect with James Ashford on social networks and say "Hi"

3. Review this book on Amazon

4. Start serving your clients to a higher level, have fun and grow a more profitable firm

48408050R00074

Printed in Poland
by Amazon Fulfillment
Poland Sp. z o.o., Wrocław